Folk

A Dolch Classic Basic Reading Book

by Edward W. Dolch and Marguerite P. Dolch

illustrated by Kersti Frigell

The Basic Reading Books

The Basic Reading Books are fun reading books that fill the need for easy-to-read stories for the primary grades. The interest appeal of these folktales and legends will encourage independent reading at the early reading levels.

The stories focus on the 95 Common Nouns and the Dolch 220 Basic Sight Vocabulary. Beyond these simple lists, the books use about two or three new words per page.

This series was prepared under the direction and supervision of Edward W. Dolch, Ph.D.

This revision was prepared under the direction and supervision of Eleanor Dolch LaRoy and the Dolch Family Trust.

SRA/McGraw-Hill

A Division of The McGraw·Hill Companies

Original version copyright © 1958 by Edward W. Dolch.
Copyright © 1999 by SRA/McGraw-Hill. All rights reserved.
Except as permitted under the United States Copyright Act, no part of this publication may be reproduced or distributed in any form or by any means, or stored in a database or retrieval system without prior written permission from the publisher.

Printed in the United States of America.

Send all inquires to:
SRA/McGraw-Hill
8787 Orion Place
Columbus, OH 43240-4027

ISBN 0-02-830814-X

3 4 5 6 7 8 9 0 QST 04 03

Table of Contents

The Three Bears

Once upon a time there were three bears. One bear was the father. Father Bear was a big bear. One bear was the mother. Mother Bear was a middle-sized bear. And one bear was Baby Bear. Baby Bear was a little bear. The three bears lived in a little house in the woods.

One morning Mother Bear made some porridge. She put some porridge in a big, yellow bowl. The big, yellow bowl was for Father. She put some porridge in a middle-sized, blue bowl. The middle-sized, blue bowl was for Mother Bear. She put some porridge in a little, red bowl. The little, red bowl was for Baby Bear.

"Let us eat our porridge," said Mother Bear.

"My porridge is too hot," said Father Bear.

Baby Bear ate some of the porridge out of his little red bowl.

"My porridge is too hot," said Baby Bear.

"We must let our porridge get cold," said Mother Bear.

"Let us go for a walk in the woods," said Father Bear.

"I like to go for a walk in the woods," said Baby Bear. "I like to see the rabbits and the squirrels play together."

"When we get back from our walk, our porridge will be just right to eat," said Mother Bear.

And so the three bears went for a walk in the woods.

While the bears were away, Goldilocks went to the little house in the woods.

Goldilocks was a little girl with blue eyes and yellow hair. She lived with her mother not far from the woods. She liked to go walking in the woods and pick flowers for her mother. And her mother always said, "Goldilocks, do not go too far into the woods."

But this morning Goldilocks had found so many pretty flowers that she had walked and walked far into the woods. She was hot and tired. Then she saw the little house where the three bears lived.

"What a funny little house," said Goldilocks. "I will see who lives in the little house. Maybe they will give me a drink of water."

Goldilocks went up to the door and called, but no one came to the door. Goldilocks opened the door and went into the little house.

There on the table Goldilocks saw three bowls of porridge.

"Oh, oh, I want some of that porridge," said Goldilocks.

Goldilocks ate some of the porridge in the big, yellow bowl, but it was too hot. She ate some of the porridge in the middle-sized, blue bowl, but it was too hot. She ate some of the porridge in the little, red bowl. Goldilocks liked the porridge in the little, red bowl. She ate it all up.

Goldilocks was very tired from her long walk in the woods. She saw Father Bear's big chair and sat down in it, but the big chair was too big. She saw Mother Bear's middle-sized chair and sat down in it, but the middle-sized chair was too big.

Then she saw Baby Bear's little chair. Goldilocks sat down in Baby Bear's chair. It was too little. Down went the little chair and down went Goldilocks on the floor.

"Oh, oh, oh," said Goldilocks, "look what I did to the little chair!"

Then Goldilocks went into the
bedroom. She saw the bears' three beds.
She got into Father Bear's big bed, but it
was too big. She got into Mother Bear's
middle-sized bed, but it was too big.

Goldilocks saw Baby Bear's little
bed. It looked just right. She jumped into
the little bed and went to sleep.

The Bears Come Home

Remember, Mother Bear made the porridge one morning and it was too hot to eat. So Father Bear and Mother Bear and Baby Bear went for a walk in the woods to let the porridge get cold.

Father Bear and Mother Bear and Baby Bear had a good walk in the woods. They came back to their little house.

"Our porridge will be just right to eat now," said Mother Bear.

Father Bear went to the table. He looked into his big, yellow bowl.

"Someone has been eating my porridge," he said.

Mother Bear looked into her middle-sized, blue bowl. "Someone has been eating my porridge, too," said Mother Bear.

Then Baby Bear saw his little red bowl. "Someone ate my porridge all up," said Baby Bear.

Father Bear looked around.

"Someone has been sitting in my chair," said Father Bear.

"Someone has been sitting in my chair, too," said Mother Bear.

"Look, look," said Baby Bear. "Look at my little chair on the floor."

"Someone is in our house," said Father Bear. The three bears went into the bedroom.

Father Bear looked at his big bed.

"Someone has been sleeping in my big bed," said Father Bear.

Mother Bear looked at her middle-sized bed.

"Someone has been sleeping in my bed, too," said Mother Bear.

"Look, look, look," said Baby Bear. "Someone is sleeping in my bed right now."

The three bears looked at Goldilocks. They did not know what to do.

Goldilocks opened her eyes. She sat up in the little bed. She saw the big Father Bear. She saw the middle-sized Mother Bear. She saw the little Baby Bear.

Goldilocks jumped right out of the little bed. She ran out of the house as fast as she could go. She ran and she ran. Goldilocks ran out of the woods. She ran right back to her mother.

And from that time to this, Goldilocks has never been to the little house in the woods again.

The Pot That Would Not Walk

There once was a big pot with three legs, and a very good pot it was. One day a man saw the big pot sitting in the store.

"That big pot is just what my wife wants," said the man to himself. So he bought the big pot and started home, carrying the pot on his back.

Pretty soon, he got very tired. He put the pot down in the middle of the road. The man sat under a tree. Then he saw that the pot had three legs.

"Big Pot," said the man, "you have three legs and I have only two legs. I think that you can carry me better than I can carry you."

The man sat down in the big pot.

"Now walk home," said the man to the pot.

But the pot would not walk.

Then the man got out and said to the pot:

"Big Pot, I will not carry you. You can walk on your three legs. Walk right along to my house."

The man told the Pot just where he lived. And he told the Pot just how to get there. And then he walked off down the road.

When the man got home, he said to his wife: "My good wife, when I was in the store today, I bought you a big pot with three legs."

"That is just what I want," said the wife. "I have always wanted a big pot. But if you bought me a big pot, why did you not bring it with you?"

"And why should I carry a big pot that has three legs? I have only two legs," said the man. "The big pot can walk to our house. I told it just how to get here."

The wife put some bread and butter and milk on the table, and they sat down to eat.

"I don't think that you bought me a big pot at all," said the wife.

"Oh, yes, I did," said the man. "And a very fine pot it is. It will be along pretty soon."

"Oh," said the wife. "Where did you say the big pot was?"

"Down the road," said the man, and he went on eating his bread and drinking his milk. But his wife got up and ran down the road.

Pretty soon she came back carrying the big pot.

"It is a good thing that you got the big pot and carried it home," said the man. "I have been thinking that it could have run away, and then we would never have seen the big pot again."

Little Red Riding Hood

Once upon a time, there was a little girl who had a long, red coat with a red hood on it. When she went for a walk, she put on her red coat. And when she went for ride with her father, she put on her red coat with the red hood on it. Everywhere she went, she put on her red coat with the red hood on it. And that is why her father called her "Little Red Riding Hood."

One day her mother said, "Come, Little Red Riding Hood. See this cake that I have made. I have put it into this basket, and I want you to carry it to your grandmother."

"Yes," said Little Red Riding Hood, "I will carry the basket with the cake in it to my grandmother. And I will be back to our house before the sun has gone down."

Little Red Riding Hood liked to go to her Grandmother's house, because her Grandmother lived in a little house by the woods. The rabbits and the squirrels played in the grass around the house. And the birds sang in the tree by the door.

Little Red Riding Hood put on her long, red coat with the red hood on it. She carried the little basket with the cake in it, and she walked down the road that went by the woods.

Now in the woods lived a big, bad wolf, and he liked to eat cake best of anything.

The big bad wolf looked out of the woods. He saw Little Red Riding Hood walking down the road carrying the basket to her grandmother.

"I think there must be a cake in that basket," said the wolf to himself. "And I am going to get it."

The wolf went down to the road. He walked up to Little Red Riding Hood.

"How do you do, little girl," said the big, bad wolf. "Where are you going with your basket?"

"I am going to see my grandmother," said Little Red Riding Hood. "I have a cake for her in my basket."

"Where does your grandmother live?" asked the wolf.

"My grandmother lives in a little, brown house by the woods," said Little Red Riding Hood.

"I can run very fast," said the wolf. "I will run on and tell your Grandmother that you are coming."

"Thank you," said Red Riding Hood. "You are a kind wolf."

The wolf laughed and ran down the road as fast as he could go.

"I will trick the grandmother," said the wolf to himself. "When the little girl gets to the little brown house in the woods, I will trick her, too. And then I will eat up the cake."

When the wolf got to the little, brown house in the woods, he went up to the door and called:

"Let me in, Grandmother. It is Little Red Riding Hood, and I have a cake for you in my basket."

But no one came to the door.

"Grandmother, Grandmother," called the wolf again.

But no one came to the door. So the wolf opened the door and went into the house.

Grandmother was not there.

The bad old wolf got one of Grandmother's caps and put it on his head. Then he jumped into Grandmother's bed.

"I will play that I am the grandmother," said the wolf to himself.

When Little Red Riding Hood got to the little brown house in the woods, she went up to the door.

"Grandmother, Grandmother," she called, "may I come in?"

"Yes, yes," called the big, bad wolf. "The door is open. Come right in."

Little Red Riding Hood opened the door and went into the house.

"I am in bed, I am not well," said the big, bad wolf. "Come here so that I can see what you have in your basket."

"I have a cake for you, Grandmother," said Little Red Riding Hood. She went to the bed and opened the basket.

The big, bad wolf looked into the basket.

"Oh, Grandmother," said Little Red Riding Hood, "what big eyes you have!"

"All the better to see you with," said the old wolf. And then the wolf put his nose into the basket.

"Oh, Grandmother," said Little Red Riding Hood, "what a big nose you have!"

The bad old wolf laughed a big laugh, "All the better to smell you with!"

"Oh-o-o-o!" said Little Red Riding Hood, "Grandmother, what big teeth you have!"

"The better to eat you with," said the big, bad wolf.

Just then the door opened. In came Grandmother and a man who was going to cut some wood for her.

"Look, Grandmother, look," said Little Red Riding Hood. "The big, bad wolf is in your bed!"

The man had a big stick, and when the wolf saw the man with the big stick, he ran out of the door as fast as he could go.

And Little Red Riding Hood and her Grandmother never saw that bad old wolf again.

The Three Wishes

Once there was a man who lived with his wife in a little house by a woods. Every day he went into the woods to cut firewood. He did not get much money for his firewood, and so the man and his wife did not have much to eat.

One day as the man walked into the woods, he said to himself:

"I work all day and I make just a little money. I am always hungry. And my wife is hungry, too."

"My good man," someone said, "I want to help you."

The man looked all around but he did not see anyone. Then he looked in the grass at his feet. And there he saw a little fairy.

"I am going to help you," said the fairy. "I will give you three wishes. Ask for anything you like, and the first three things that you ask for, you will get."

Then the fairy was gone. The man ran back to his house as fast as he could go. He wanted to tell his wife the good news right away.

"Wife, wife," he called, "come here, for I have good news to tell you."

His wife came running. "Tell me, tell me," she said. "What is the good news?"

"I was walking in the woods," said the man, "and a fairy called to me. She said, 'I will give you three wishes. Ask for anything you like, and the first three things that you ask for, you will get.'"

"We can wish for anything that we want," said the wife, "and it will come to us?"

"Yes, let us sit down and think of the things that we want to wish for," said the man. "I am hungry and so let us have something to eat."

The wife put some bread on the table. The man and his wife sat down to their little table. And they talked as they ate.

"Just think, wife," said the man, "we can ask for much, much money. And then we can buy everything that we want."

"Yes," said the wife, "we can ask for a big, big house."

"We can ask to be a king and queen," said the man.

"We could ask for children," said the wife. "I have always wanted many children. We could have five boys and five girls."

And so they went on talking and eating. Soon all the bread on the table was gone. The man was hungry and so he said:

"I wish that I had a big sausage," and there was a big sausage on the table.

"Oh, oh, oh," said the wife, "now what did you do that for? You wished for that old sausage and now we have only two wishes."

"I was so hungry," said the man, "that I did not think. I just forgot and made a wish for something to eat. But we have two more wishes. We could ask for much, much money. And we could ask to be a king and a queen."

But his wife said over and over again:

"I do not see how you could have wished for that old sausage. Why did not you think before you made a wish? Just think of all the things we could have had if you had not wished for that old sausage. I do not see how you could have wished for an old sausage."

Now, the man wanted his wife to stop talking about the sausage.

"You talk too much," the man said to his wife.

"Talk too much!" said the wife. "You are the one who talks too much. Just look at that old sausage on our table."

"Sausage, sausage, sausage!" said the man. "Will you stop talking about that sausage? I wish that sausage were on the end of your nose."

All at once the sausage was on the end of the wife's nose.

"What have you done?" said the
wife, who could not get the sausage off of
her nose. "What have you done to me?"

The man did not know what to do.
He tried to pull the sausage off his wife's
nose. But he could not get it off.

"We have one wish," said the man.

"I will ask for much, much, money
for you. Then you can have anything
that you want."

"But everyone will laugh at me with a sausage on the end of my nose," said the wife.

"I will ask that you be a queen," said the man.

"What good will it do me to be a queen?" said the wife. "Everyone will laugh at me with a sausage on the end of my nose."

The man did not know what to do.

"I only wish that the sausage were not on the end of your nose," said the man.

And all at once the sausage was gone.

The man and his wife were right back where they started. They had no money. They had no big house. They had no children. They were not a king and queen.

The sausage was gone. And they had no bread in the house. And so the man walked back into the woods to cut some more firewood.

The Little Red Hen

A pig and a dog and a cat went to live with a little, red hen. They all lived together in a little, white house that was on a hill. One day the little, red hen found some corn.

"Who will help me plant this corn in my garden?" asked the little, red hen.

"Not I," said the pig.

"Not I," said the dog.

"Not I," said the cat.

"Then I will plant the corn myself," said the little, red hen. And she did.

The corn grew in the garden. First, the corn looked like grass. The corn grew and grew. Pretty soon the corn was yellow. Then it was just right to make into cornmeal.

"Who will help me cut the corn?" asked the little, red hen.

"Not I," said the pig.

"Not I," said the dog.

"Not I," said the cat.

"Then I will cut the corn myself," said the little, red hen. And she did.

Now it is hard work to cut corn. And the little, red hen got very, very tired.

"Who will help me make this corn into cornmeal?" asked the little, red hen.

"Not I," said the pig.

"Not I," said the dog.

"Not I," said the cat.

"Then I will make the corn into cornmeal myself," said the little, red hen. And she did.

The little, red hen worked and worked. Pretty soon she had some corn meal.

"Who will help me make this cornmeal into bread?" asked the little, red hen.

"Not I," said the pig.

"Not I," said the dog.

"Not I," said the cat.

"Then I will make this cornmeal into bread myself," said the little, red hen. And she did.

The little, red hen made the cornmeal into corn bread. And then she baked the corn bread. And, oh, how good the corn bread smelled when it was baking!

The pig smelled the corn bread baking and came to the door. The dog smelled the corn bread baking and came, too. The cat smelled the corn bread baking and came to the door. And, oh, how good the corn bread smelled when it was baking!

Pretty soon the corn bread was done. The little, red hen put the corn bread on the table.

"Who will help me eat this corn bread?" asked the little, red hen.

"I will," said the pig.

"I will," said the dog.

"I will," said the cat.

The little, red hen looked at the pig and the dog and the cat.

"You did not help me plant the corn," said the little, red hen. "You did not help me cut the corn. You did not help me make the corn into cornmeal. You did not help me make the cornmeal into corn bread. And now I will eat the corn bread myself." And she did.

The Fox and the Bag

Once upon a time an old fox found a bee. He put the bee into a big bag that he carried on his back. And off down the road he walked.

The old fox went to a house where a woman was by the door.

"My good woman," said the fox, "will you be so kind as to keep this bag for me?"

"Yes," said the woman, "I will keep your bag for you."

"Thank you," said the fox. "I shall be back soon. But do not look into the bag." And the fox walked off down the road.

When the fox was gone, the woman said to herself, "I wish that I knew what was in that bag. I shall take just a little look."

The woman opened the bag and out came the bee.

The fox came back and saw that the bag had been opened.

"Where is my bee?" asked the old fox.

"I opened the bag," said the woman, "and the bee got away."

"Then I must have your red rooster to put into my bag," said the fox.

The fox put the red rooster into his bag and off he walked down the road.

The fox went to a house where a woman was looking out of the window.

"My good woman," said the fox, "will you be so kind as to keep this bag for me?"

"Yes," said the woman, "I will keep your bag for you."

"Thank you," said the fox. "I shall be back soon. But do not look into the bag." And the fox walked off down the road.

When the fox was gone, the woman said to herself, "He said not to open the bag. But I wish that I knew what was in it."

The woman opened the bag and out came the red rooster.

The fox came back and saw that his bag had been opened.

"Where is my red rooster?" asked the fox.

"I opened the bag," said the woman, "and the red rooster got away."

"Then I must have your white pig to put into my bag," said the old fox.

The fox put the white pig into his bag and off he walked down the road.

By and by, the fox saw a man working in his garden.

"My good man," said the fox, "will you be so kind as to keep this bag for me?"

"Yes," said the man, "I will keep your bag for you."

"Thank you," said the fox. "I shall be back soon. But do not look into the bag." And the fox walked off down the road.

When the fox was gone, the man said to himself, "I wish that I knew what was in that bag."

The man opened the bag. The white pig jumped out of the bag and ran away.

"I think that old fox was going to eat that pig," said the man to himself. "It is a good thing that he ran away." And the man went and got his big, brown dog and put him into the bag.

When the fox came back, he did not think that the bag had been opened. He put it on his back and went off down the road.

The sun was hot, and the fox got very tired. He sat down under a tree.

"I think," said the fox to himself, "that I shall eat this little pig right now." The old fox opened the bag and out jumped the big, brown dog.

Oh, how that old fox ran. He ran, and he ran, and he ran. And the big, brown dog ran right after him. And no one ever saw that old fox again.

The Seven Men of Gotham

One day seven men of Gotham went down to the river to fish. Two of the men got into a little boat and went out on the river to fish. Three of the men got into a big boat and went out on the river to fish. And two of the men walked in the grass by the river and fished.

The men fished all day. They caught many fish. And when the sun was going down, the men in the little boat came back. And the men in the big boat came back. And the men who had walked by the river came back. They came together under a tree by the river.

It had been a good day for fishing. The men showed the many fish they had caught. "We had better be getting home before the sun goes down," they said.

But one of the men said, "Are all the men here?" And he began to count.

"One, two, three, four, five, six. There are only six of us here. One of us has fallen into the river, for this morning seven of us went fishing."

Another man started to count. "One, two, three, four, five, six. Yes, I count only six men here."

Now all of the men thought that one man had fallen into the river. They ran up and down the river looking for the man who was gone. Some of the men went out on the river in the little boat. And some of the men went out on the river in the big boat. They looked and they looked, but they could not find the man who was gone.

The men came together under the tree by the river and they said, "Now we must go home for the sun has gone down." And so the men started down the road carrying their many fish.

And coming down the road they saw a man riding on a white horse.

The man stopped and said, "Good day to you, my good men. I see that you have many fish."

"Yes, yes," said the men, "we caught many fish today. But one of us is gone. Seven of us went fishing. But now we can count only six of us who are going home." And one man counted again, "One, two, three, four, five, six."

"What will you give me if I find the man who is gone?" asked the man on the horse.

"We will give you all the money we have with us," they said.

"Let me count you then," said the man.

"One, two, three, four, five, six, seven," he counted. "There are seven men here, all carrying fish," he said.

"There were only six men when I counted," said one of the men.

"There were only six men when I counted," said another man.

"One, two, three, four, five, six, seven," counted the man on the horse again. Then the man on the horse laughed and laughed.

"The man who counted did not count himself," he said. And away he went down the road.

The Gertrude Bird

In a town far away, there once lived a little, old woman with red hair called Gertrude. She lived all by herself. No one ever went to see her and tell her the news of the day. Gertrude liked to talk to no one in the town. Gertrude cooked and baked, but she never gave any little cakes to the children in the town.

One day Gertrude put on her black dress and her white apron. Then Gertrude made a cake. It was the best cake that she had ever made. And just as she was about to sit down at the table and eat her cake, a little, old man came to the door.

"My good woman," said the little, old man, "I was just walking by your house and I smelled your good cake. May I have some of your cake to eat?"

Gertrude looked at her cake on the table.

"This cake is too big to give to you," said Gertrude. "Come in and sit down by the fire, and I will bake you a smaller cake."

The old man went in and sat down by the fire. And Gertrude made a little cake. She put it into the oven to bake. And when the cake was done, it was bigger than the cake she had made for herself.

"This cake is too big to give to you," said Gertrude. "Sit by the fire, and I will make you a little cake."

The old man sat by the fire. And Gertrude made another cake. She made it just as small as a cake could be. She put it into the oven to bake. And when the cake was done, it was the biggest cake of all.

"This cake is too big to give to you, my good man," said Gertrude. "You had better be going on your way, for I have no cake to give to you."

The little old man got up out of the chair and went to the door. A light was all around him.

"Gertrude, Gertrude," said the little old man, "you do not know me. I am the fairy that sits by the fire. I like those who are kind. You are a selfish woman, Gertrude. I do not like selfish women."

The little, old man went out of the door, and Gertrude never saw him again.

Then Gertrude sat down at her table to eat her cakes. But Gertrude had no hands to eat with. Gertrude was not an old woman—Gertrude was a redheaded woodpecker.

And when you see a redheaded woodpecker, you will see Gertrude's black dress and white apron. She lives in the woods now and she does not eat cake. She has to work very hard to find anything to eat. She picks and picks and picks away at the trees all day long.

The Three
Billy Goats Gruff

Once upon a time there were three
goats who lived on a farm. One was
Little Billy Goat Gruff. And one was
Middle-sized Billy Goat Gruff. And one
was Big Billy Goat Gruff.

The three goats liked to eat green
grass. And every day they wanted to go
over a little bridge. They wanted to eat
the green grass that grew on the other
side of the bridge.

But in the water under the bridge lived a troll. He was a little man with big, big eyes, and a long, long nose. And this troll liked to eat little goats.

One day Little Billy Goat Gruff said, "I think that I will go over the bridge and eat the green grass that grows on the other side."

Little Billy Goat Gruff went over the bridge, "trip, trap, trip, trap."

"Who is that tripping over my bridge?" called the troll.

"It is I, Little Billy Goat Gruff," said the goat.

"I am coming up to eat you," called the troll. The troll looked over the side of the bridge with his big, big eyes.

"Oh, please don't eat me," said Little Billy Goat Gruff. "I am so little. Let me go over to the other side of the bridge and eat the green grass. Then I shall grow bigger and bigger."

"Get along, then," said the troll.

The Little Billy Goat Gruff tripped over the bridge, "trip, trap, trip, trap." And he ate the green grass that grew on the other side of the bridge.

Pretty soon Middle-sized Billy Goat Gruff said, "I think that I will go over the bridge and eat the green grass that grows on the other side."

Middle-sized Billy Goat Gruff went over the bridge, "Trip, Trap, Trip, Trap."

"Who is that tripping over my bridge?" called the troll.

"It is I, Middle-sized Billy Goat Gruff," said the goat.

"I am coming up to eat you," called the troll. And the troll looked over the side of the bridge with his big, big eyes.

"Oh, please don't eat me," said Middle-sized Billy Goat Gruff. "I am not as big as I shall be. Let me go over the bridge and eat the green grass that grows on the other side. Then I shall grow bigger and bigger."

"Get along, then," said the troll.

And the Middle-sized Billy Goat Gruff tripped over the bridge, "Trip, Trap, Trip, Trap." And he ate the green grass that grew on the other side of the bridge.

Pretty soon Big Billy Goat Gruff said, "I think that I will go over and eat the green grass that grows on the other side of the bridge."

Big Billy Goat Gruff went over the bridge, "TRIP, TRAP, TRIP, TRAP."

"Who is that tripping over my bridge?" called the troll.

"It is I, Big Billy Goat Gruff," said Big Billy Goat Gruff.

"I am coming up to eat you," called the troll.

"Come right along," said Big Billy Goat Gruff.

The troll with his big, big eyes and his long, long nose got right up on the bridge. Big Billy Goat Gruff put his head down and he butted that troll. He butted that troll right off of the bridge. He butted that troll right into the water. And no one saw that troll again.

And every day the three Billy Goats Gruff went over the bridge. They ate all the green grass that they wanted. They grew bigger and bigger.

a	bed	carried
about	bedroom	carry
after	beds	carrying
again	bee	cat
all	been	caught
along	before	chair
always	began	children
am	best	coat
an	better	cold
and	big	come
another	bigger	coming
any	biggest	cooked
anyone	Billy	corn
anything	bird	could
apron	birds	count
are	black	counted
around	blue	cut
as	boat	day
ask	bought	did
asked	bowl	do
at	bowls	does
ate	boys	dog
away	bread	done
baby	bridge	don't
back	bring	door
bad	brown	down
bag	but	dress
bake	butted	drink
baked	butter	drinking
baking	buy	eat
basket	by	eating
be	cake	end
bear	cakes	ever
bears	called	every
bear's	came	everyone
bears'	can	everything
because	caps	everywhere

eyes	goat	hot
fairy	goats	house
fallen	goes	how
far	going	hungry
farm	Goldilocks	I
fast	gone	if
father	good	in
feet	got	into
find	Gotham	is
fine	grandmother	it
fire	grandmother's	jumped
firewood	grass	just
first	green	keep
fish	grew	kind
fished	grow	king
fishing	grows	knew
five	Gruff	know
floor	had	laugh
flowers	hair	laughed
for	hands	legs
forgot	hard	let
found	has	light
four	have	like
fox	he	liked
from	head	little
funny	help	live
garden	hen	lived
gave	her	lives
Gertrude	here	long
Gertrude's	herself	look
get	hill	looked
gets	him	looking
getting	himself	made
girl	his	make
girls	home	man
give	hood	many
go	horse	may

maybe	pig	showed
me	plant	side
meal	play	sit
men	played	sits
middle	please	sitting
milk	porridge	six
money	pot	sized
more	pretty	sleep
morning	pull	sleeping
mother	put	small
much	queen	smaller
must	rabbits	smell
my	ran	smelled
myself	red	so
never	redheaded	some
news	remember	someone
no	ride	something
nose	riding	soon
not	right	squirrels
now	river	started
of	road	stick
off	rooster	stop
oh	run	stopped
old	running	store
on	said	sun
once	sang	table
one	sat	take
only	sausage	talk
open	saw	talked
opened	say	talking
other	see	talks
our	seen	teeth
out	selfish	tell
oven	seven	than
over	shall	thank
pick	she	that
picks	should	the

their	tripped	white
then	tripping	who
there	troll	why
they	two	wife
thing	under	wife's
things	up	will
think	upon	window
thinking	us	wish
this	very	wished
those	walk	wishes
thought	walked	with
three	walking	wolf
time	want	woman
tired	wanted	women
to	wants	wood
today	was	woodpecker
together	water	woods
told	way	work
too	we	worked
town	well	working
trap	went	would
tree	were	yellow
trees	what	yes
trick	when	you
tried	where	your
trip	while	